Self-Portrait with Ghosts of the Diaspora

Meghan Sterling

Harbor Editions
Small Harbor Publishing

Self-Portrait with Ghosts of the Diaspora
Copyright © 2023 MEGHAN STERLING
All rights reserved.

Cover art by C. R. Resetarits
Cover design by Allison Blevins
Book layout by Allison Blevins and Ellie Davis

SELF-PORTRAIT WITH GHOSTS OF THE DIASPORA
MEGHAN STERLING
ISBN 978-1-957248-15-8
Harbor Editions,
an imprint of Small Harbor Publishing

To Adeline and Matthew, always
To my family, who taught me everything

Contents

Gifts / 9

Because, In Fact, We Are the Ghosts / 11

Thief / 12

Scar / 13

My Grandfather Wouldn't Speak of the Old Country / 14

Letter To Miami Beach After a Condo Collapse / 15

Legacy / 18

The Night Sea Dreams / 18

Self-Portrait with Quilt and Synesthesia / 19

I Am Craving the Moon's Disappearance / 20

Motherhood Divides a Woman in Half / 21

Self-Portrait with Ghosts of the Diaspora / 23

What the Knife / 24

Rosh Hashanah / 25

The Weight of a Cumulonimbus is One Million Tons / 26

One Morning When We Rose Early / 27

Rabbit Rabbit / 28

With Her Gone / 30

Just Behind My Shoulder-Blades, Some Dry Thing,
    Wide-Eyed, Gently Closes / 31

What the Trees / 32

Coping Mechanisms / 33

Still Here / 34

Self-Portrait with Ghosts of the Diaspora

Gifts

I sit at this table, crumbs fallen
from my grandmother mouth
decorate the wood with its dry lace,
empty jars stacked in the pantry—
borrowed from my grandmother fear
that everything of use must be kept
as a talisman against poverty—drawers
full of costume jewelry in soft silk bags
hedged from my grandmother desire,
beauty at any cost—as long as it's cheap—
rhinestone glamour, satin bosom, patent
leather shoes with buckles—hear the call
of trains with my grandmother dread,
smoke that falls up into a sky
a flat white stone, rows and rows
of flat white stones—guard against the past,
a past only allowed to visit in dreams.

*

Because, In Fact, We Are the Ghosts
After Stephen King

and know this—ghosts are patient. Skin of rotting
soil, hair of crumbling stone. Their fingers like the edge

of a spade. How they see with eyes open what we see
with ours closed. Ghosts have a way of staying overlong—

my grandmother's face in the mirror, a lover dead from heroin
circles above the dining room table, a boy from 8th grade

crawls the skin of my forearms. In the house where I
grew up, they live in fan blades, air conditioning vents,

patches of moonlight along the floor in white tetrahedrons.
Ghosts like pets. I trip over them when they wander underfoot.

I scrub them out from under my fingernails, rake their dirt
with the end of my pen. They follow me out to the garden

but can only make little hills of earth in the beds. They follow
my scent, come with me on planes. They wait in the vestibule

for the toilet like quiet children. They try not to take up space.
At dawn, they stand together at the edge of the roof, balance

on the gutter, look down at the empty street while
the streetlights soften, necks craning to see the ocean.

Thief

I can taste it on my teeth—the only real freedom
is the white page and black pen, the only relief
the wine I've drunk in the middle of the day
that allows me to sleep half the afternoon and
the snow white ice and the wind off the river, cedar
trees each standing in naked winter dignity with
little white hats on the tip of each
branch, and the salt of sleep I haven't tasted since
before my daughter was born, the way sleep
was unburdened and easy and replenishing instead
of the haunted half-sleep now, full of watchings
and wakings and vigilance, full of guilt and dreams
about everything I've ever stolen or wanted to,
rubies from a catalogue, my grandmother's opal
brooch, beef jerky from a convenience store, o,
the horror when I found it in my hand a block
down the road, my hand clutching it tight, how
I ran from the invisible police, how I am running still.

Scar

Willing herself steel on the tenement rooftop

where the pigeons roosted and ate crumbs

from her hands, near dusk she watched

their steady flight above cracked brick

and the washing snapping against lines

in flags of gray with blue beyond and refused

to come down for dinner, my grandmother

showed me the scar where her mother's frantic knife

sailed across a plane of water towers and steam

and plunged into her 4-year-old back, where slanted metal

angles crossed a horizon lilac with smoke, New York's

metal wires and iron gates, chimneys and the tippy buses

crawling along the Brooklyn Bridge on their knees

and one small fingernail slant of moon.

My Grandfather Wouldn't Speak of the Old Country

not the mud streets in the ghetto or the sound of bombs,
not the crumbs scattered across the table like stars,
not the rooms where every night he saw his breath hover
above his bed like his spirit leaving his body. My grandfather
wouldn't speak of his broken back or the scar on his wrist,
not the girl in the Kalitsky shtetl in 1941, not the last time
he saw her behind a wire fence. He didn't tell me about the snow
that fell so fast it flew upwards, nor the way it blew under
the kitchen door and striped the floor, not his thin shoes
or constant cough. Not the planes that whirred their tin
engines just above the patched roofs, not the day his father left,
not the dead in the ditch. My grandfather did not talk about
the long walk into Kyiv to buy bread, how he kept his head
down the whole way, and he didn't tell me of his dreams about
his mother's face, coal where her eyes should have been.

Letter to Miami Beach After a Condo Collapse

Dear Sinking City, when my grandparents arrived,
you were a small strip of sand sandwiched between
swamp and jungle, mosquitos thick as wolf's
fur, the trolley letting people off on a Lincoln Road that
was barely a farm stand of stray lettuces. Dear Ancestors,
how came you to the end of America? Here it was they
decided to sell their wares—shoes and clothes, dungarees
for the workmen draining the swamps and fighting off
the alligators in the Everglades. Miami, you stacked
my forebears into apartments, while the clouds like
lowering tongues stayed near the earth, the sandy loam,
pockmarked grass banks and artificial hills soft with heat.
The ocean was always looming, a monster, green-scaled,
mouth bigger than any alligator. Its mouth could swallow
all of their dreams if they had let it. Their alligator handbags
and matching pumps. Their new Mercedes with the camel
seats. Soon, the trolley would take them down a road lined
with shops, your Baker shoes, your Richards Department Store,
your condos multiplying, crawling over each other like bugs
in heaps of sand. Dear Miami, dear Sunset, how is it
your condos survived the hurricanes, your condos
layered like a pastel cake a thousand miles deep? Your condos
wearing down like teeth. Your condos coming down in the night,
breaking into sand and dust, rushing to meet the ocean who waits.

*

Legacy

Times I scuttled near the roots of the rowan,
barking my one lean song. Times I crouched.
Times I crept. How often I waited for nightfall
to become the sound I most feared, the garbled
tongue, music from the mouth of the fox, the bear.
My mouth, blurred with all I had never spoken.
I wept into the grass that turned dark as my wished-for
fur, tufts scented in sex. How my throat
would cough up its need to the wind as I followed
winter's trail—its one crooked finger pointing along
the frozen ground toward the houses and their beds
of nails, toward mothers and their half-starved dreams.
How I slunk to etch my story in the frozen trunk.
How it healed itself into the shape of my name.

The Night Sea Dreams

That silver dawn bears no weight, its last wooly leaves
are fire coral sunk to the bottom of the branch worn bare.

Night coming early bears no weight—at five p.m. the day
shuts closed like a clam's stony mouth. My daughter calls for me,

and I begin to weave the narrative of motherhood: the matted
wool woven around our ankles, an ancient's net tied to the bed

for an oyster's life span. This is not only metaphor. My daughter
calls for me from her bed, her voice an unworn splinter, an arrow

in the dark, a skein. Over and over the cat walking across our bodies
in gray shadow, like me, unable to settle, unable to rest. Awake

to my daughter's shouts as if falling into water, night air
a whip to the face. Without moon, I can't see what isn't here.

Plum picked clean as the seafloor. Mirror of the night sky washed
in red yarn. Mirror of my daughter's photograph. Pearl's blue light.

Self-Portrait with Quilt and Synesthesia

Tell me again why we came here,
this land of pine and water with its scent
of undone stitching, all of us busy
with our children and gardens. *My kale
did nicely this year. July was wet and stormy,
the tomatoes drowned.* I woke up this morning
and the sunrise looked like a bowl of scrambled eggs.
I wade through shadows with my fingers
to find words to comfort September's
rainfall, write so I can contain myself
in a cup of tea, small as a thimble on the tip
of a mouse's tongue. Tell me why every morning
aches like the color lilac, why sleep is racked
with dreams of the earth's bright end. Tell me why
my daughter shivers like a dandelion against
a blowing mouth, why my daughter in the night
sings out all her generation's acquired terror.
Tell me again why I inherited the bad stomach,
why I see my father blurred in the mirror before
I've put on the makeup that hides the resemblance.
Tell me why fog tastes like raspberries, the trees
laugh in the clouds with their little hidden
leaves, the morning fallen down and sleeping.
Tell me why my story isn't the same story
lived by those before me, wading through
the dark into more dark, now that I've lost the thread.

I Am Craving the Moon's Disappearance

and a silence as deep as an oil well, thick with black crude,
petrol that coats the walls, dulling sounds to hollowed drum.
I am craving an enormous tub of scented milk where I float
in a ring of flowers and there's no voices or light, and I have
no skin raked raw with nerves traveled to the surface
like the bones of ancient animals, my ribcage as big as a boat
exposed to the glare of a midnight sun in some blowing desert
wind. Just last night, my nerves grew outside of my body like thin
vines, wrapped my skin tight as a bow. My daughter played them
with her crying, my husband with his questions. The kitchen light
poked them with its yellow fingers, the texts with their little black
letters like thorns. I am craving emptiness, relief from the clamor
of metal and wood and gravity and morning and people who want
my attention and body and time, who call it love.

Motherhood Divides a Woman in Half

where one part is snow on the forest floor, shadow shape
of the crescent moon, leaf fall and beetle scurry, the night

calling with a voice lean as the wolf, still puddle full of cloud.
Here I live alone with fire, search the dung heaps left by the elk,

scratch poems in the mud with a branch mottled with frost.
This part I've never been able to follow to its end—the way

of earth's deep musk, the way of fragrant berry. I
always turn back and take up the mantle of the other, the one

who sits vigil in the room while my daughter sleeps, where I am
sentry, lifeguard, loon, riding the water with my daughter clinging,

through waves that send their pulses to the edge of the shore, where
I paw at the water, where I paddle our bodies so we stay afloat,

where the only silence is underwater, where solitude is a looming tangle
of forest always a distance ahead, lit by hunger, lit by sun.

Self-Portrait with Ghosts of the Diaspora

The discomfort is my guide. It takes me down
into the theatre of the past, into my dreams of the shtetl,
my dreams of the earth seen from a space shuttle,
hazy green and blue, the last colors before drowning.
It keeps me dabbing ink at a tongue that rolls off
the wrong phrase—how I jabber on, out of nerves,
out of a longing to connect my dot to your dot where
our dots make a jumble of static. The discomfort leads me
into myself, under thinning flesh, where the bones of my family
are lodged like toothpicks in my teeth after a big meal,
where the circles under my family's eyes roll like hoops
down a Brooklyn Street, where the Yiddish my family spoke
rises like dots to the thought cloud I carry over my head
repeating itself ad infinitum: *belong, belong, belong.*

What the Knife

told was the future, that I was deep into the dream
until I wasn't, grasping a two-handled knife
with five blades, slicing at the sky and from the tear,
rain sluiced across the fish-white of my forearms,
leading me into storefronts, their torn blue awnings,
finding myself in a glittering shop in New York
where I looked into a mirror and brought my hands
to the sides of my face, loving what I saw as if
for the first time, as if I were staring into the face
of my own child. I woke up confused, a shadow
of the love I felt for myself like a pillow over my breath—
why am I in this bed? Who is this man beside me?
Why is there a slant bar of light beneath a shade
drawn nearly flush to the sill? Coming to, I felt
the ache of my own empty mouth, felt the skin
on my face as one I have worn with regret, how
I resembled so many dead, how I wished I could
carry the tenderness I felt for myself in the dream
into my life, mothered myself gently, gently, cradled
the knife, releasing its switch and finding a flower.

Rosh Hashanah

A Jew without a house, a houseless Jew, a Jew without
worship. *Shana Tova*. The fruitcake in its wrapper,
the Rabbi's wife on the stairs. I work until my hands

and eyes go numb, and the work is a pile of bricks
where a house used to be. Happy New Year to the indigo
dawn. Happy New Year to the carpal tunnel, the Eustachian

tube dysfunction. Happy New Year to the ten extra pounds
since forty, to the harried, harrowing evenings chasing time
and dinner and clean countertops while my daughter

barks orders like a German general in a bad Nazi movie.
Highchair tyrant. Toddler dictator. Meanwhile, the fields
are calling. Casco Bay islands in little beaded chains off

the coast sit like clams in the sand. The sun grimaces
with its gold mouth. The earthquakes shake loose the sun's
gold teeth. Happy New Year to the hurricanes casing the joint,

searching for change in the cracks of the floor. The hurricanes
like a Jew drowning to get the quarter nailed to the pool's bright
bottom—that old Finnish joke, the synagogue in Helsinki

a deep red brick and shuttered. What did my grandmother
say? *A Jew without a temple is like a Jew without jazz, a Jew without
a grandmother, a naked Jew.* Improbable. Lost.

The Weight of a Cumulonimbus Is One Million Tons

Morning is a drawn-in breath. Morning
is an old boat, drummed out of its mooring,
left to sink or drift. The dread inside the shell,
the mantle and its empty rainbow. The dawn shatters
lilac, lavender, colors of an old woman's scarf.
Just last night I dreamt I was older, my skin and hair
bleached in desperation, made late to my own wedding
by the madness of a flock of sheep, their white bodies
stretched down the road in an endless sky, an unwound scarf.
I woke up to darkness and felt relief. Then I remembered.
Morning breathes me like the weight of a cloud
suspended in air despite its million pounds. Morning
floods my chest with something like light. Morning
is a ticking clock, the place where my face and the face
of my father merge in a composite of grown man, oyster shell,
cloud full of rain, time too short to call anything mine.
I have forty minutes until my daughter breaks into my room,
her body sticky with last night's urine. I have forty minutes
to dream I am holding the shell of dawn in my hands before
it is broken like a plate.

One Morning When We Rose Early

Memory of her voice on the phone in the dark as we planned
for a sunrise over the Catskills, and the next day as I waited

for the light to come over the hill, for her to come and be
the light before the light. This was before I understood

that wanting comes from somewhere hurt. Her breasts
like the bed I wanted to die in, her voice like the color green,

her face like the harvest moon, dipped in wax. I wanted to touch
her body the way I had wanted to be touched by my mother—

gently, just before sleeping, sexless as stones. I waited on the hill
and she came near dawn as she said she would, came under my blanket

to warm ourselves as the sky bloomed from navy to white, the last star
holding stubborn to watered silk. She came and shivered with me

and the icy sun and we sang rounds, me and this mother I had made
for myself out of flesh and cloth, here in the Great Lonely North.

Rabbit Rabbit

November first and all is wet stone, one day
closer to quiet, one day farther from childhood.
Last night was Halloween and ghosts, running
streets in taffeta and lace, light and dark
like twins with their hands held out in tight fists.
Which will you choose? I choose flame from shadow,
the moon blotted by bright cloud, how the moon
is the face we wear now. What fire it hides.
Dawn so dark this morning, paired stars offer
their tined light like cigarette burns in cloth,
eye holes in a velvet mask we think is sky,
and I am balanced in the center of this saw,
how one day soon, it will tilt. One day burn.
Like all things, the end comes with teeth bared.

With Her Gone

I swept myself under the rug with the rose petals
and bees, winter heavy as my grandmother's Persians.
The wood ash smearing my wrists. The wood pile
listing to the left, still green, still too wet to burn.
The resulting smoke always filled the house, and I
would open the door to let in the icy air like the tips
of many bladed tongues. I would lie on the couch alone
and watch the night come like a wave to fill my mouth
with its weight, to stirrup my mouth with its dark rope.
Grandmother was gone, and so was my reason, my blue ribbon.
Grandmother was gone, and autumn came like a flick
of a whip, and then winter, with its long slow hours of nothing
but wanting her back. Grandmother was gone.
I turned to shadow, and there was no moon.

Just Behind My Shoulder-Blades, Some Dry Thing, Wide-Eyed, Gently Closes
Virginia Woolf, on drinking wine to sleep

I can dream myself into small forgettings,
this body like lead, this body like stones
in the pockets of Virginia Woolf, all night
awake, the River Ouse calling. Without the gift
of sleep, the hours bark like dogs, the hours trip
on their own feet, the hours become water that stills,
then stops, forms a puddle to look down into
and grow surprised at the face that looks back.
I've begun to see the end. It is far yet, but has shape,
light around the edges, ridged and smooth as sea glass.
Water will bring it to my feet, like wood carried to shore
by the waves. When I dream, I dream all this is enough.
The wood. The water. The occasional sleep that delivers
its delicate pearls to my mouth.

What the Trees

The trees say *plait*. They say *plage*. The wind shreds
their skin, the wind wears them down, opens space

between the tangled branches. They say *light*. They cling

to the last yellow leaves like a badge of loss. They say *less*.
They wear the scent of rain in their disappearing hair.

The trees' bodies weave a wall between our lives in the street

and the woods. They make an edge where the woods are something
seen beyond a roofline. Someplace where birds go to live.

The trees point their branch tips at the garbage collectors.

They shrug their shoulders at the blue sky tossing itself
like seeds. They swear last year was different. I plan to be

different. I plan to touch the trees today. I will look them in the eye.

The trees don't mind me, it's the weight of their years
that bends them. They struggle to stand upright. They breathe

into our mouths. They say *heat*. They say *home*. They say *hold on*.

Coping Mechanisms

Succor, meaning honey stirred into the bitter slurry
of our morning tea, when we pray we can more
than stumble, more than carry all that's tasked to us;
meaning the meager hand I offer my daughter
when she stirs in the night, afraid of all the dark
might hold—spiders in the web of shadow cast
by the window grilles, zombies in the filaments
of the digital clock numbers long on the wall;
meaning the frame of light around the door we breathe
to nearness, its yellow symmetry, its four thin stripes
against night pigmented with the memory of blood;
meaning the spools of quilting thread my grandmother
wound and rewound, the strand tight against the meat
of her palms, sewing with fists clenched in impatience
with men; meaning the waves beneath the boat as my grandfather
floated out into the blue horizon stretched thin as wire, eager
for the business of fish on the line and the miles between him
and the unmade beds. Succor, meaning years of forgetful sleep
ripe with silence against the buzzing of appliances and moon
on the floor; meaning the ghosts we think we see in the hinges,
in the cracks beneath the windows and the curtains blowing thin
as milk; meaning the moon heavy in the trees, the moon
and its withered apple face.

.

Still Here

Death is only a little bit of something.
The shadow of the cat on the blanket,
the sliver of light between the curtains
as the sun rises over the scabby earth.

Life is only a little bit of something.
The sky also. My daughter asks if the sky
will end, and I say yes, it becomes space
outside the earth's skin. She asks if she fell

in space how long would she fall. Only a little bit,
only until ever, until always, falling alongside
all our ghosts who never landed. We are always
falling a little bit, maybe a lot.

I start to tell her that and then stop myself.
Yesterday evening, too tired, I fell sideways
into the cabinet, her milk catching my wrist
in three white drops like phases of moon.

I am too tired at night—my hands begin
to fumble and weaken. It is a little death,
to feel my body give way like this, the bottle
in my hand until it isn't, the milk for her bedtime snack

dousing my wrist as if anointing me in the little bit
of her she still is, still my daughter not a little
but a lot, how she looks like my grandmother
and still fits in my arms

and wants her milk in a sippy cup before bed
though my wrists weaken and drop it at night
when I am tired of holding myself upright
against the delicious pull of gravity in this life

with its little bit of death mixed in, this life
where if I fell I would just keep falling
through sky like a sliver of light between curtains,
like three drops of milk on my wrist,

how my daughter's
voice rasps like my grandmother's,
like a crack of light shining across
the floor in a dark room to announce that it is day
and it is morning and we are still here.

Acknowledgments

Grateful acknowledgment is made to the editors of the following journals, who published these poems, or earlier versions of them:

Anti-Heroin Chic: "One Morning When We Rose Early"
Birdcoat Quarterly: "Legacy"
Boats Against the Current : "Gifts"
Cantos: "With Her Gone" and "Just Behind My Shoulder-Blade"
Fine Print: "My Grandfather Wouldn't Speak of the Old Country"
Leon Literary Review: "The Weight of a Cumulonimbus Is One Million Tons"
Mudroom: "What the Knife"
Rappahannock Review: "Motherhood Divides a Woman in Half"
South Florida Poetry Journal: "Letter to Miami Beach After a Condo Collapse"
Subnivean: "Self-Portrait with Ghosts of the Diaspora" and "Still Here"
The Café Review: "Self-Portrait with Quilt and Synesthesia"
The Idaho Review: "Because, In Fact, We Are the Ghosts" and "Hashanah"
Whale Road Review: "What the Trees"
Willawaw Journal: "Scar"

Meghan Sterling (she, her, hers) lives in Maine. A multi-Pushcart nominee, her work can be found in *The Colorado Review, The Los Angeles Review, Meridian, Rhino Poetry, Hunger Mountain, Nelle, Radar, The Idaho Review, Solstice*, and many others. *These Few Seeds* (Terrapin Books, 2021) was an Eric Hoffer Grand Prize Finalist. Other collections out in 2023*: Comfort the Mourners* (Everybody Press) and *View from a Borrowed Field* (Lily Poetry Review's Paul Nemser Book Prize). She is the Program Director at Maine Writers and Publishers Alliance. Read her work at meghansterling.com.

www.ingramcontent.com/pod-product-compliance
Lightning Source LLC
Chambersburg PA
CBHW051705040426
42446CB00009B/1321